HO'

YOUTUBE CHANNEL

FOR BEGINNERS.

Learn how to Create, Edict, Optimize and upload videos to your YouTube channel.

Stanley P. Cathcart

LEGAL DISCLAIMER

This book and its content provided therein are for information purpose and to serve as a guide on how to make additional income with YouTube channel. All information in this book is deemed accurate as of the time of publishing. However, this is not an exhaustive treatment of the subject, and expert opinion may differ.

Any use, of this book, is at user's risk, the author does not assume and at this moment disclaims any liability to any party or any loss, damage caused by errors or omission resulting from accident, negligence or any other cause.

This book intends no guarantees of income or profits. Many variables affect each individuals result. Your result will depend on how you correctly apply the knowledge and how committed you are to your job. The author does not accept responsibility for your outcome. If you wish to use the ideas contained in this book, you are taking full responsibility for your choice, action or result.

CONTENTS

Stanley P. Cathcart...1

LEGAL DISCLAIMER i

INTRODUCTION..v

CHAPTER ONE 1

Reasons you should start a YouTube channel today. 1

CHAPTER TWO 15

What kind of channel do I run? 15

CHAPTER THREE...29

How to set up your YouTube channel professionally. 29

CHAPTER FOUR 42

Define your audience..42

CHAPTER FIVE 53

Getting familiar with your audience 53

CHAPTER SIX..58

Producing high-quality videos. Value-based and content. 58

CHAPTER SEVEN..65

Getting your video equipment for less than $90......................65

CHAPTER EIGHT...74

Editing your videos with Shortcut free software. 74

CHAPTER NINE 92

How to upload your video 92

CHAPTER TEN..100

Optimizing your YouTube channels. 100

CONCLUSION...118

HOW TO START A YOUTUBE CHANNEL FOR BEGINNERS. STANLEY P.
CATHCART

INTRODUCTION

YouTube was established in 2005 and bought over by Google in 2006. It is the world's most prominent video distribution social network, the second biggest search engine, and one of the topmost three websites globally. Viewers watch hundreds of billions of hours of video on YouTube every day. Many of them go on to like, comment, and distribute the video to their friends. YouTube's viewers tilt in the direction of the younger people but also reaches more adults aged 18 to 49 than any cable network in the world. It can link businesses with a vast audience.

People are attracted to YouTube for its distinctive content and public which allows them for networking in ways that are not possible with traditional channels such as television. It is free and simple to use, turning it into a valuable marketing tool.

Once you create a branded YouTube medium, you can begin sharing information and networking with audiences, permitting them to build allegiance for their channel.

Businesses can also pick up what their viewers are saying by observing the comments. YouTube analytics can track the performance of a medium and its videos with current statistics about engagement, views, demographics, and more.

YouTube can be an enormously effective channel for sales crews to inform users about products and services. For marketing crews, video puzzles about future product releases can produce excitement and inspire conversations.

Businesses and individual can leverage YouTube's added features such as cards and end screens to entice audiences to view more content, increase public engagement, get new subscribers, and inspire a specific call to action to be carried out.

As we move into how to make money with YouTube channels, we will be covering this

HOW TO START A YOUTUBE CHANNEL FOR BEGINNERS. STANLEY P. CATHCART

subject in three-part books which I am encouraging you to get three of them to get a balanced knowledge on how to run a successful YouTube channel.

CHAPTER ONE

Reasons you should start a YouTube channel today.

In this chapter, we will be considering some of the cons and pros of starting a YouTube channel. What is on YouTube that you should devote your time to it? What is the pro and cons of not just starting a YouTube channel but taking YouTube seriously, even as a career choice, or as something you want to build side part-time or even full-time income from?

But let's start with the negatives and its downside.

1. YouTube is ultimately a long game. That's right; YouTube is not a quick place

to make some cash. It is a marathon, not a sprint. So, I would agree in the short term that just for everybody, that you're going to make a lot more money from doing other jobs, another career, or other work. However, YouTube is a long game, and if you have patience and persistence, you can find that not only your income can grow, but other benefits of YouTube can outweigh the upfront work that you have to put in.

2. Competition is rising. It is true that a lot of people want to be on the platform. Whether as a way of making side income or even as a way they build their other businesses. And so people are trying to claim digital real estate, but I think it can be overcome and that if you can figure out how to be different and you're very strategic, you can still break through.

3. The YouTube learning curve. You know, in another career you may be just the editor. Not to minimize that, but you do one thing. You might edit, and that's what your job entails. When you step into the YouTube arena, you become everything. You become the visionary, the editor, the

shooter, the designer for thumbnails, the SEO specialist for writing the text in the descriptions, the social media expert for sharing your videos on social. And not that you have to learn all that stuff at once, but there is quite a bit of learning curve of how to shoot video, how to be on video, how to edit video. And so, a lot goes into it, and I think that holds people back at times.

But it is overcome able. If you commit to lifelong learning and skill development, I believe that one by one anybody can add the different skills necessary for success on YouTube.

Those are some of the negative sides to consider if you should start a YouTube channel or not. So let's jump into five quick reasons why I love YouTube the most and why I think you should too.

1. YouTube is the second largest search engine in the world. Now, this is an enormous deal. That means that second to Google where people go for looking for, "How do I fix my car?" Or "Where's the best restaurant?" Or "How do I make more money in my business?" Or "How do I lose

belly fat without dieting?" And they ask a million different questions in Google.

The second place people turn to for answers is YouTube. This is a game changer for discoverability. And so my question is if you're trying to grow your influence on Facebook, on Instagram, on Snapchat, these platforms don't have as much discoverability opportunities. Your hope is that you show up on a featured page or that somebody shares your content or that you got to pay for ads. But because YouTube is a search engine that means that you can grow your influence and get discovered by people who don't know you yet. Simply by showing up on the other side of people's questions.

I believe that this makes YouTube one of the leading platforms to ultimately grow your influence if you're willing to develop the skills and put in the necessary work.

2. YouTube channel brought freedom. For entrepreneurs, freedom is one of our highest values, isn't it? To be boss, to be able to work on your terms. To be able to show up to work when we want to and work on what we want to.

And so, one of the things that I love the most about YouTube is that it is a blank canvas. And you get to be designing the content, the way you want to run your business, when you upload your videos, what kind of content you upload. It is a dream for entrepreneurs or what I like to say is videopreneurs. And over time, you can build up multiple streams of income.

So, I've had YouTube replace the income that I would make from having a full-time salary job or even from doing freelance work. YouTube has been able to not just match that but exceed that over time.

3. YouTube channel helps you join an amazing community. Whether you're creating content or not, you're already participating in this YouTube ecosphere. You're seeing how cool it is that people are meeting in the comments.

I have met some of the most important people in my life on the internet. It's pretty amazing and in this YouTube community. And I find that I draw a ton of inspiration over like-minded people that I meet at YouTube and social media platform. When we have this shared passion for online video, for creative freedom, creativity, and collaboration, I found that YouTube is an incredible community and it's worth being part of it and contributing to as a creator.

4. YouTube is becoming mainstream and legitimate. A lot of a people, if you were to tell them that you were a YouTuber, you were pursuing a YouTube career, most people will still think you're crazy. They would think, "What do you mean?" That place where people upload cat videos and viral videos. "What do you mean you're thinking about a YouTube career?" I mean, even friends and family still don't understand what I do.

But the reason I feel like that's a huge opportunity and why you should consider starting a YouTube channel now is because I would say that YouTube isn't fully mainstream yet, but it's getting there. Some of the signs that we're seeing is smart TVs, right? The YouTube app and game consoles are just integrated with a lot of people's way that they watch content. Even the usual way they would traditionally watch cable television or network television.

Beyond that, YouTube launched YouTube TVs, a competitor with DirecTV, Cox, and other things. And so YouTube is becoming more and more mainstream. I think that's important because now is the time to plant your flag. People who put in the hustle put in the work, and invest what it takes to build their influence, to build an audience on YouTube right now, will be positioning themselves for a lot more mainstream success in the coming years.

5. YouTube channel has a massive opportunity. Now I know there's increasing competition, but Susan, the CEO of YouTube, recently announced that YouTube has over 1.5 billion monthly logged in users that are watching over an hour of content per day on YouTube with their mobile devices. And that's just logged in users.

That means the consumption is much, much larger than that. Additionally, a recent Huffington Post article talked about the rising billion of new consumers that are coming online between now and 2020.

Talking about three to five billion new people are going to be coming online over the next few years, causing the greatest surge to the global economy that we've ever seen.

And so, when I think about these things, I think there is competition on YouTube, but there's still massive opportunity. If you could figure out how to be different, how to stand out, and if you're strategic in the way that you post videos and you position your videos, it is still one of the best places online to grow your influence.

So those are just a few of the reasons on why to start a YouTube channel. And I was writing from the standpoint of somebody who may have the desire to pursue YouTube full time. But the one other thing I would say is I also think that YouTube is a great place to build up a side project or a side hobby, especially for creative people. If you're a creative person, even if your job involves creativity, I think we all need a side project as creators.

And YouTube is a great place to earn a little side income, have a little fun, upload some videos, and maybe get some free products, work with some companies, work with some brands. Even if it never becomes your primary source of income, I think there's so much opportunity in running a YouTube channel.

And I found that those who have stayed committed and have built their influence haven't regretted the subscribers that they've built, the lessons they've learned along the way, and the opportunities that have come their way from starting and committing to a YouTube channel.

6. Everybody lives an entirely different life even if they're in the same city or they have the same job as somebody else. No one lives the same life in the same way, and I think that everybody has something to share with the world because we all have different values, we all have different dreams, and we can learn something from everybody. So, even if you feel like you don't have a lot to share, people are going to like you because of you and not because you're doing something cool or whatever.

They want to see you have something to share daily whether it's a favorite quote or

HOW TO START A YOUTUBE CHANNEL FOR BEGINNERS. STANLEY P. CATHCART

maybe it's a way that you live your life, or maybe you don't drive a car, and you use public transportation. To me, that's so cool because I live in a city where I have to drive a car but I love watching people who use public transportation and don't have to own cars, I think that's the coolest thing.

I think you should start a YouTube channel because you have something different to offer that nobody else does.

7. It helps you to be creative. So, I think that having a YouTube channel has been a super awesome creative outlet for me. If you are a creative person but maybe right now you don't have a way to express your creativity, a YouTube channel is an awesome way to do that and still be able to inculcate it into your life right now. I am trying to be creative about shots that I'm getting, trying to change it up a little bit,

I'm always thinking of what else could I do, how could I be different, how can I be better? And I'm still going about with my day; I'm working two jobs today. So, it's still a part of my life but I'm able to be creative at the same time, and it's something to think about. You're always going to be thinking about how you can be better and what else you can do and what other ideas that you have.

I think it's an awesome way to be creative if you are a creative person and it helps you even to be more creative when you're in it, and you're doing it all the time, you are continually coming up with new ideas.

8. You will learn a lot about yourself. You will challenge yourself. The more you film and the more topics that you talk about you will start to recognize what you like and what you feel mediocre about. So, you will start to learn and the more you do and learn, the more you will realize what's important to you. That's what's happened to me.

I've realized what I love talking about, and then there are other things that I always thought I'd be interested in and I wanted to do, but I don't enjoy sitting down and talking about those things. Now, I can prioritize the things that I love.

It's also going to be a challenge. You're going to be challenged to make videos that you don't like, maybe a subscriber or many subscribers are going to ask you for a certain video that you're not super comfortable filming or you don't know that you're super interested in. You still want to make those for your subscribers because they are loyal to you, and they watch you and they're just genuinely interested in your life. You will be challenged to make videos that maybe you don't enjoy so much. You're going to have to do things that you might not like so much and that might be a little bit harder and more challenging for you but that's how we grow I think it's necessary.

9. It gives you so much self-confidence. If you don't play the comparison game or you at least get past the comparison game because we all compare ourselves to other people, especially on social media.

It's tough because a lot of times you only see the best in everybody and you're only seeing them at their happiest moment and when they are doing something that is so exciting and that they love. You're not seeing them on the days when they're working or the days when they feel down or anything like that.

It's easy to compare yourself to other people thinking I'm not doing as good, why am I not as happy? Once you get past all of that, that's when you start to shine because you realize nobody is like you, you're just going to do your thing, whatever makes you happy. However making videos makes you happy, you still have a completely different personality than anybody else. You are a completely different person than anybody else, and that's what makes you unique. You can't compare yourself to others, and you can't base your life after seeing only the best pieces of somebody else's life.

You should do what makes you joyful, and you have to talk about what makes you happy. No matter what it is that you're doing people are going to like you because of who you are as a person. And when you just let your real true personality come out, and you do what you love, people are going see that; they're going to be able to see that you're so passionate about what you're talking about or what you are doing.

HOW TO START A YOUTUBE CHANNEL FOR BEGINNERS. STANLEY P. CATHCART

And that's when your personality shines. People are going to love you because you are you, no matter what you're doing or what you're talking about in your videos. It's helped my confidence a lot, and it's something that you have to jump in and do. If you don't start doing it, you're going to overthink it, and overanalyze it, and try to have everything perfect. But if you don't start doing it, you're going to have a hard time figuring out who you are on YouTube or social media. You have to get started and experiment with different things and grow and learn as you go.

CHAPTER TWO

What kind of channel do I run?

In this chapter, I will be giving you tips on how to start your own YouTube content. We will look at some existing YouTube, what they offer and how you can learn from it. These sites are only to give you ideas on what is possible on YouTube. You can model them and start your own YouTube channel today.

In today's world, everything can go on YouTube as long as it will benefit your viewers. Are you trying to come up with an idea for a YouTube channel or maybe you're trying to level up and rebrand your existing channel? We have got some YouTube channels that hopefully may encourage you to find your ideas for your channel.

One way to connect with your community is to go in your analytics, you go to the community tab, and you can see who is subscribed to your channel. All the channels we will be talking about prove just two things to you:

1. You can make a channel just about anything you know. YouTube is so big, don't limit yourself to what you see. There are channels about everything. We're going to talk about some of them.

2. Having a clear focus can be very powerful and let get right into it right now.

Some channels that will give you ideas on how to start your own YouTube channel today are:

1. DailyEffectivePrayer:

The image above shows you how the channel looks. It's a channel that teaches about prayers. When you click on videos, you will see all kinds of prayers that the YouTuber prayed. You can turn to this channel for a prayer of thanksgiving, morning and evening prayers, prayer for new homes, prayers for jobs, etc. This shows us clearly that if you have passion for anything you can put it on YouTube. Here is the link to the YouTube video in case you want to learn more about the channel.

https://www.youtube.com/channel/UC8Cd Bdhgb-RLWj2dB_VPCyQ/featured

2. bleepinJeep.

Taking a look at the image above you will see clearly how this channel looks. From checking out, this channel has done an excellent job here, and again this is proving that you can make a channel around your passion and it demonstrates that people are going to care. If you are consistent, you can build up momentum around one theme. Go here to learn more about the channel.

https://www.youtube.com/user/bleepinjee p

3. Michel New

This is a channel that teaches how anyone can learn piano very well. This is how the channel looks like:

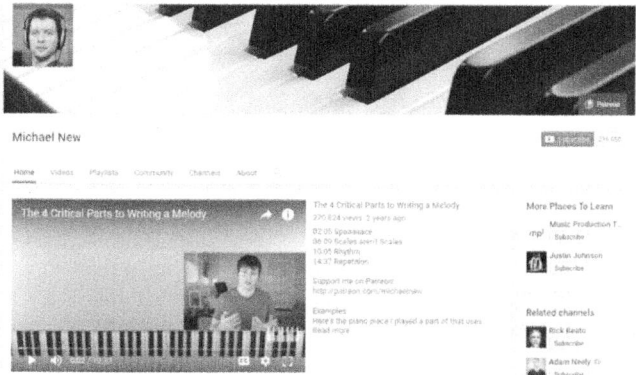

I like this channels because I am a music lover and I play the piano a bit too. This site is an excellent resource for whoever wants to be good at playing the piano. You can see that Michael has taken his passion to YouTube and has thought so many people how to play piano too. As you can see, he has built a very massive audience of music lovers. You can also click on the about me link and read more about the YouTuber. Here is the link to the channel.

https://www.youtube.com/user/Rhaptapsody/featured?disable_polymer=1

4. Engineered truth: Here again is another great channel that you need to learn from, take a look.

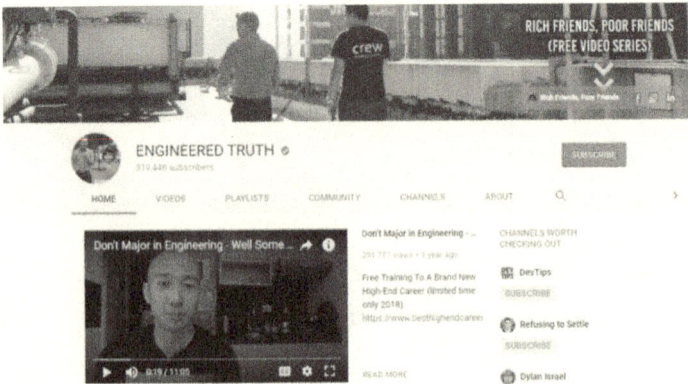

What I love about engineer truth is that he's talking about different career choices that maybe not everybody knows and you know what I like about him is that he's hitting on a point that a lot of people struggle with which is like what do I want to do with my life. And he's helping you explore other options than just going to school. So, his channel serves a particular group of people with a challenge that he was trying to help you with. Learn more here https://www.youtube.com/user/Engineere dTruth

5. Mihran Kirakosian. This channel teaches how to dance. It is such a fantastic channel.

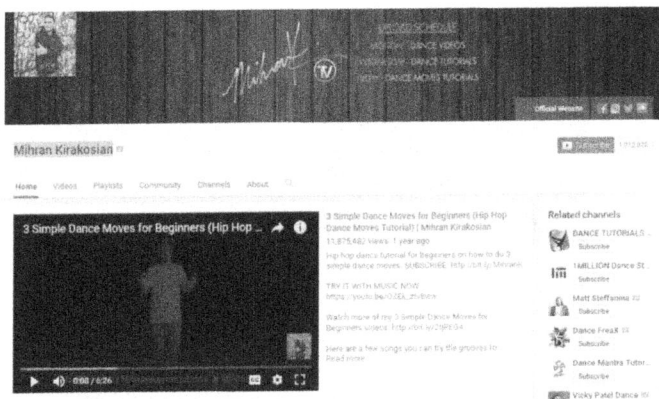

Do you have a passion for dancing? Do you like watching people dance? This is another excellent channel that will entertain you and at the same time teach you step by step on how to dance if you want to dance and don't know how to do so. Click on this link to view the site and learn more. https://www.youtube.com/channel/UC-ZaFVre7Koir_VcaM2LpNA

6. Biffa. You can see from the image below that this is a beautiful website to behold and learn from.

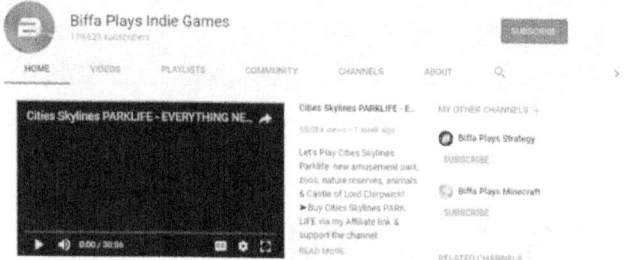

So, one of the things that we talked about a lot is the power of not just niching once but multiple time. And with much channels the gaming space, is super crowded right? But he's gone very specific and specifically strategic building games and has carved out this community around one type of gaming inside of the larger gaming world. This link takes you to the channel to learn more.

https://www.youtube.com/user/Biffa2001

7. Millionaire Hoy. Another excellent channel to behold with a beautifully made banner.

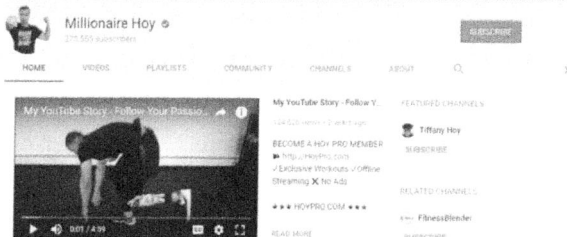

This is an inspirational fitness channel. I Love your channel, Millionaire Hoy. What I love about it is the fact that you've combined inspiration with fitness. Now we know that fitness is a massive thing on YouTube in general. But of the fact that you like to inspire people to get them motivated to get fit I think is impressive. Another thing I love too is the fact that this channel do shout out to the local community, so it has some events that people in the Chicago area can attend. A lot of people there are so focused on the global reach; they forget that sometimes it's even more powerful to meet people in person, what you can do in your community. Absolutely! We can learn something from this channel because you've got a new workout Sunday through

Friday at 3 pm PST. So, we always talk about conditioning your audience and being consistent.

8. Everyday tactical videos: Just taking a look at the channel you will know what to expect, take a look.

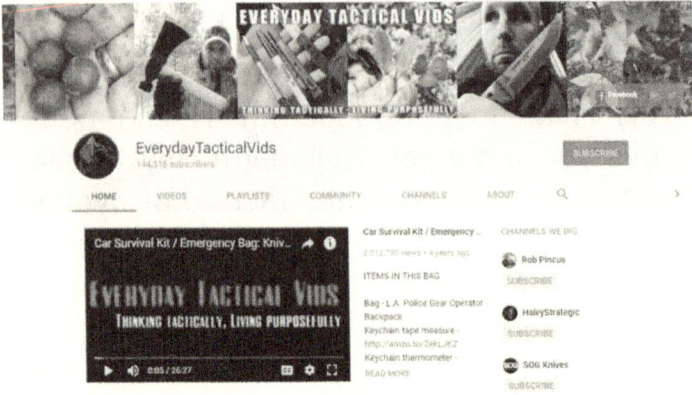

This is an excellent channel, is a survival theme, thinking tactically and living purposefully. And as soon as you get to this channel you get that vibe, you see survival knives being reviewed backpacks. You see these kinds of tips. Building a channel around your passion keeping it focused.

All these channels are targeted and unique. It shows that you know what you are most passionate about. What could you turn into a YouTube channel but that stays on a brand as these channels do? Do you want to go to the channel? Go here https://www.youtube.com/user/EverydayTacticalVids

9. Weavers of eternity.

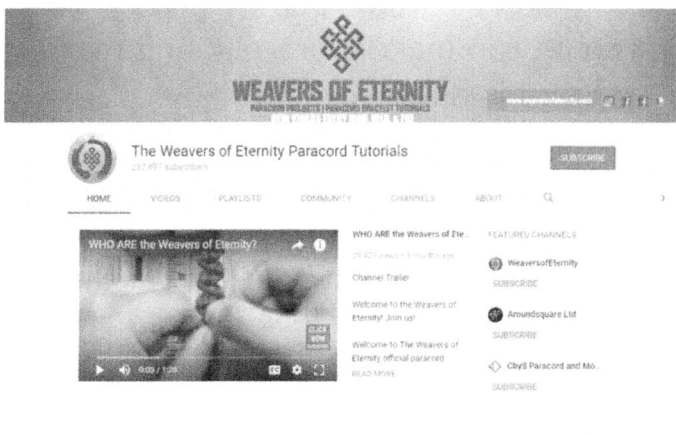

I love this channel; I love that it is teaching people how to make paracord bracelets. And a couple of things I love about this channel

A. This channel proves that you don't have to be on camera. I know the YouTuber show up in the videos but all his

HOW TO START A YOUTUBE CHANNEL FOR BEGINNERS. STANLEY P. CATHCART

thumbnails are his final product, and that's cool.

B. Themed video. In addition to just making these super dope bracelets, this channel sometimes picks up a theme to design the brace around. And that's great for ranking. You know people into Pokémon can make a bracelet and make it look like a Pokeball.

People that are into marble can find a specific character for example x-men and make a bracelet around the x-men colors they can give it that Marvel theme. I love this channel; I love how creative it has been with something that a lot of people would perceive as being simple. What is cool with this channel in particular is, there are different ways to monetize your channel especially when you have a very focused niche like this. Weather through affiliate marketing of Paracord, we're not sure about everything that this channel is doing, whether through sponsorships and websites that focus on Paracord. And that's true for jeeps, fitness, or indie games, so many different opportunities. Once you build your influence, you also start building your income.

10. Suck my mod. Looking at this channel, you will glean some lessons.

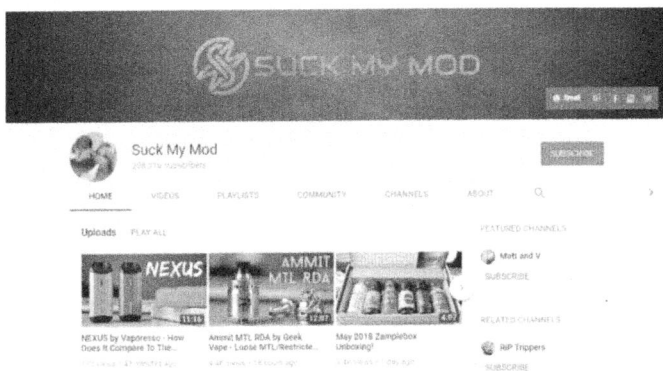

This again is another way to prove that you can build any YouTube channel about something you're passionate about. It was cool to read from the about page of this channel that the YouTuber was a traditional smoker for many years he transitioned and then build a YouTube channel. I want this video to inspire you to take anything that you're passionate about and put it on YouTube.

I think it's powerful again that these are very specific, so Matt and Vanessa are doing different flavors and different tools.

27

And when you start going deep into a niche, you find that it goes super deep. One of the things I love about that is the fact that you're not just doing product reviews, but you have ranted about vaping right.

There are so many different variations around vaping that you guys have created videos on and you have not limited yourself to just doing product reviews. I have shared these channels to illustrate the power of taking your passion and putting it on YouTube. Also the power of being focused. Just jeeps concentrate on fitness and inspiration. How can you focus your current channel, whereas you're starting a channel to build a powerful niche?

In this chapter, we have looked at ten channels that should inspire you and propel you to start your own YouTube channel today.

CHAPTER THREE

How to set up your YouTube channel professionally.

Your YouTube channel is a lot like a refrigerator. You might have a lot of content, but if nobody knows where it is, they're not going to watch it. The idea behind this chapter is that even if you have fantastic content if you don't set up your channel so that people can easily find that content, nobody's going to watch it.

You don't need anything special to have a YouTube channel; all you need is your Gmail. Once you have a Gmail, you can head over to youtube.com and sign in.

Click on "**SIGN IN**" where the arrow on the image below is pointing at and sign in.

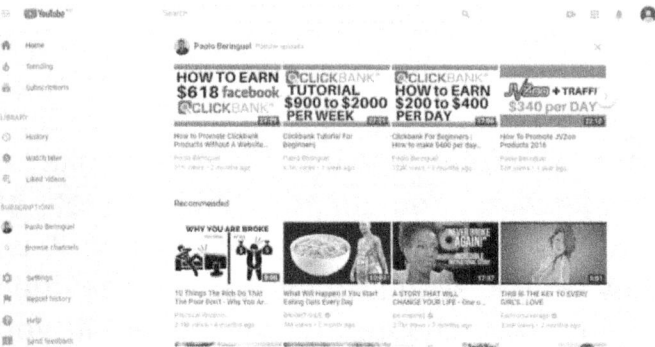

Once you sign in, you will find the page that looks like what you see in the second image above. Then click on the image icon at the top right of the page.

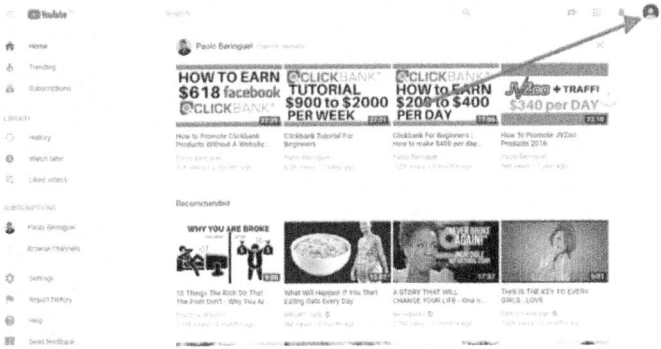

When you have clicked on that icon, it will bring out a drop-down menu which you need to select My channel.

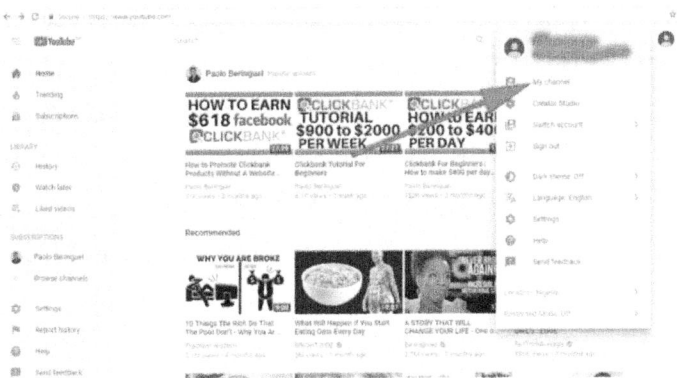

After selecting "**My channel**", it will bring you to the page that will enable you to create your channel. You will see this:

Use YouTube as...

Learnarea

By clicking "Create channel", you agree to YouTube's Terms of Service. Learn more
Changes you make here may show up across Google services with content you
create and share, and to people you interact with. Learn more
Use a business or other name

CANCEL   CREATE CHANNEL

Go on and click on "**CREATE CHANNEL**" to create your channel after you must have filled in the name you want your channel to have. Without this, you cannot upload videos to YouTube.

In this case, I name this new channel we are working with as **learnarea**. Whatever name you decide to give to your channel is up to you.

Let's move on. Once the channel is created, you will find this next page.

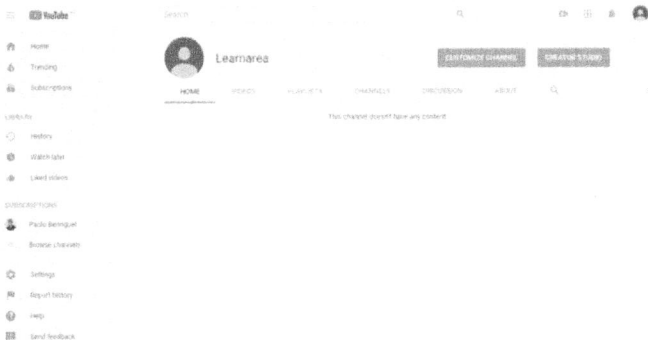

As you can see from the image above, the channel does not have any content yet. You can add your photo or any other picture you want to use as your profile picture here, and you can also add a banner to your YouTube video.

Adding a profile picture to your channel.

While you are still on the page shown above, you will see two blue taps to the right of the page. One of them is "**CUSTOMIZE CHANNEL**" while the other is "**CREATOR STUDIO**". To add profile pictures to your channel, you need to click on the "**Customize Channel**". You can also change the profile picture directly by clicking on the circle with an image in it close to the name of this channel. It will

33

take you to the photos on your computer then choose the one you will like to use for the profile picture. But using the customized channel tap helps you to change profile picture and banner of the channel.

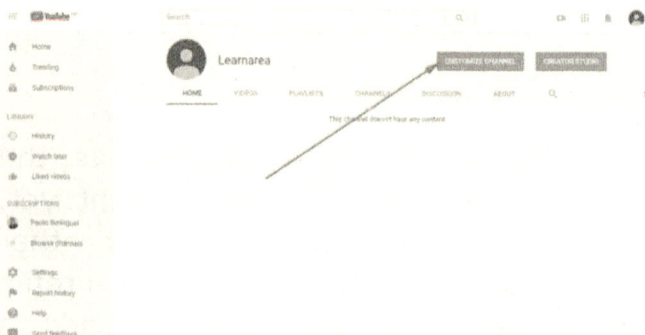

When you click on the "**CUSTOMIZED CHANNEL**" tap, you will land at this page.

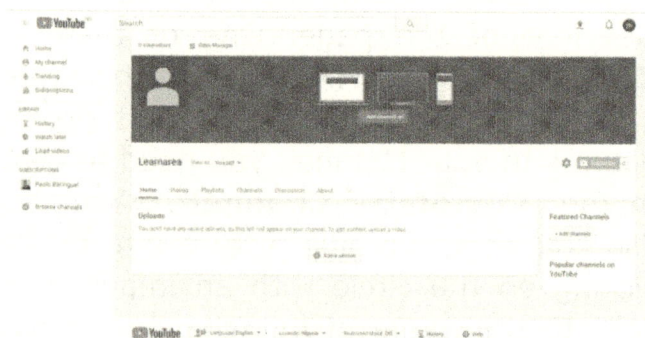

Click on the human portraits image to the left of the page and add profile picture to your channel.

Adding a banner to your channel.

Still, on the same page above, click on "**ADD CHANNEL ART**". When you do that, it will bring you to the page below.

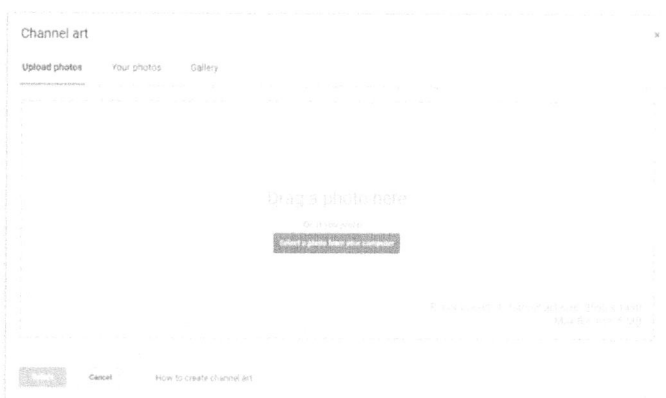

Click on "**SELECT A PHOTO FROM YOUR COMPUTER**" at the middle of the page and pick a picture you want to use as your banner from your computer. In this example we are working with, I have added a profile picture and a banner to the page as you can see below.

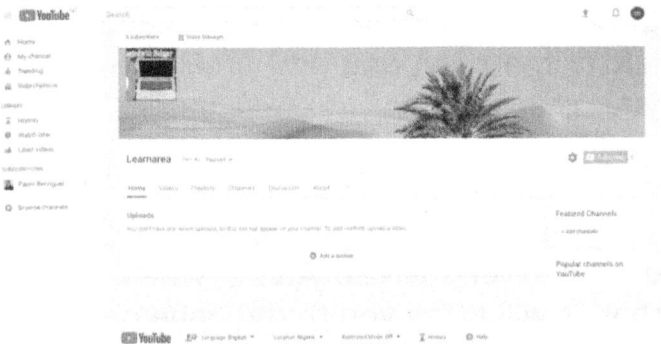

Note: Be always professional with the mages you use whether it is a profile picture or a banner. Make sure your Banner shows clearly what your page is all about. Let your banner start delivering the message you want to pass across to the public first.

In the examples above, I used all the images for learning purpose only, so I was not mindful of the kind of image I used. If you know, you cannot design your Banner professionally by yourself. You can head to fiverr.com where a professional will do it for you for as low as $5.

Customizing your playlist.

There are different layouts you can choose from whether it is a horizontal or a

36

vertical arrangement, this depends on how you want to set up your playlist and what form you chose. To be able to set up your playlist this way, you must be uploading videos regularly.

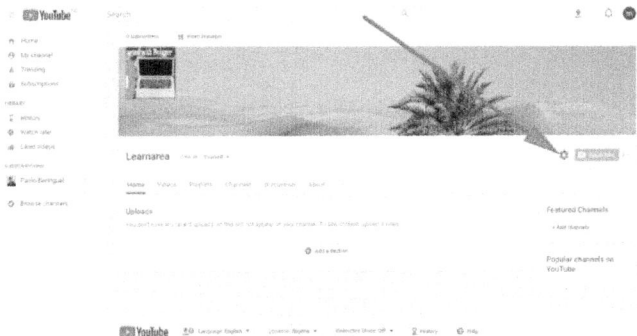

Click the setting Button where the arrow is pointing at.

Channel settings

Privacy

Keep all my liked videos private

Keep all my subscriptions private

Keep all my saved playlists private

Access more options in Account settings

Customize the layout of your channel

Recommended for people who upload videos regularly. Add a channel trailer, suggest content for your subscribers, and organize all your videos and playlists into sections.

Access more options in Advanced settings

Show discussion tab

Allow your fans to comment on your channel.

Display automatically ▾

Translate info

Reach audiences in foreign countries by translating channel info.

Cancel   Save

You will land at this page, and then use the "**CUSTOMIZE THE LAYOUT OF YOUR CHANNEL**" to do your settings. You will have to click on "**ADVANCED SETTINGS under CUSTOMIZE THE LAYOUT OF YOUR CHANNEL**" to do your settings. Once you are done with the settings you desired, click on save and your settings will be saved.

Adding content to the ABOUT page

What tells people what your page is all about is what you put on the about page of your YouTube channel. If you leave it, blank people cannot say what your YouTube is all about when they visit your channel. The about page here is crucial. It is your first selling point for whoever visits your channel, so it will be wise to write good content on your about page. People like relating with individuals they know and they can trust, your center of trust is the ABOUT page of your channel. Just click on the "**About**" tap inside your YouTube channel.

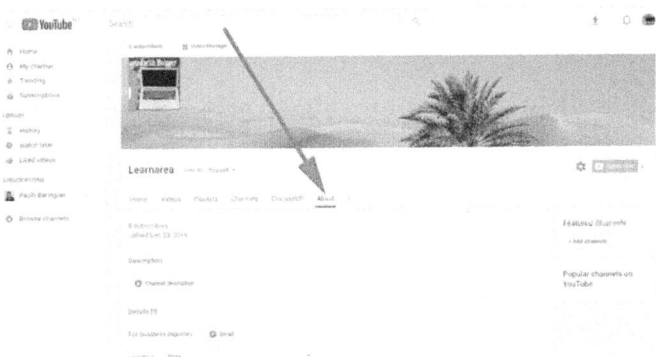

When you click on that tap, it will land you on this page.

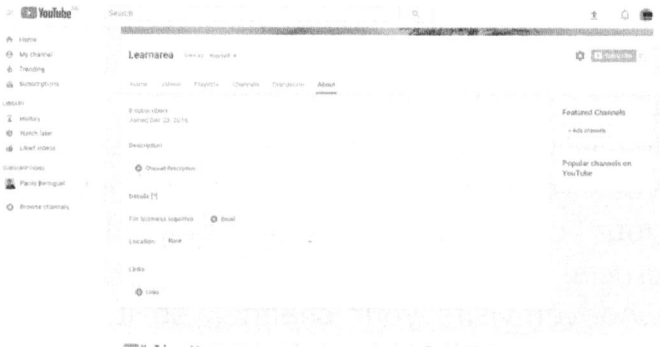

Do all the necessary settings the way you will want it to be and save it. You need to click on the plus sign beside the **"CHANNEL DESCRIPTION"** tab and put a description about your channel. This is where people get to know what your channel is all about.

Put in the email that you will want people to contact you with. Some people would like to reach you with questions bordering them, with your email they would be able to do that.

Also, set the location of your channel or where you are located. You can see the tab there too.

Another important thing you need to do here is adding links to your channel. You have the right to add up to 5 links to your channel. There could be your blog link, your social media link, your affiliate link or whatever link you will like your viewers to click on and see.

Once you are done with all these settings, your page is alright and ready to go live. You can go on and learn how to publish great videos that will get you tons of views, and you can go ahead and monetize it. You can make a full-time income from YouTube if you are diligent enough to work it out.

There are no shortcuts to life's most significant achievements. The secret to success in life is hard work and consistency.

HOW TO START A YOUTUBE CHANNEL FOR BEGINNERS. STANLEY P. CATHCART

CHAPTER FOUR

Define your audience.

In this chapter, we will be discussing the personality types that are likely to watch your channel. This is important because you might be monetizing your channel and understanding your viewers will help you determine the kind of advert you should place on your channel. Now, this may not be a one-fit-all method, in any case, you have to do your common sense analyses too, but this will guide you on how you can decide what to advertise on your channel. In part two and three of this book which you should be looking out for, I will be talking entirely about how to use tools provided by YouTube to get more views and how to monetize your channel.

In those books, I will show you how to use analysis to decide what kind of advert to place on your YouTube channel. For many of us reading this book now, we may want to go into affiliate marketing to make some money from there too. A YouTube analytical tool helps you to decide on what kind of product will suit your audience and how to advertise it to them effectively. So, let's dive straight into what we have for today and see how Psychographics can help us analyze our audience.

Psychographics involves classifying people according to their values, beliefs, opinions, and interests. So, it's very much about their personality. It's mainly qualitative data as it's difficult to count like quantitative data but generally more detailed and more in-depth. Most psychographic profiles are built from people in the advertising industry. They do however relate to the media, but they talk about the audience as consumers and buyers rather than media watchers or listeners. It's still a great way to classify an audience.

For example in this list developed by the advertising agency Young & Rubicam called cross-cultural consumer characterization or foursie's for short, we can see psychographic categories. Now, these categories might seem to be based on unfair and judgmental stereotypes which may seem offensive, but they are used by the advertising and marketing industry to summarize groups of individuals. So let's go through these more closely and consider the types of media product that these people might consume, and also what advertising we might see within these programs to confirm what we notice.

THE RESIGNED

These people are rigid, strict, authoritarian and have chauvinistic values, they're oriented to the past and resigned roles. Their brand choices generally stress safety, familiarity, and the economy. So, the newspaper this person might read would be something like the Daily Mail. The television they might watch would be relatively simple crime dramas such as Inspector Morse. And we can confirm this

HOW TO START A YOUTUBE CHANNEL FOR BEGINNERS. STANLEY P. CATHCART

through the types of advertising we see within these media texts and the types of adverts we see in those papers. In this case a particular type of car cruises, insurance and so on. Although this description suggests an older male, it could just as easily be a female with slightly different programs of choice and therefore adverts.

THE STRUGGLER

These people are alienated, struggling, disorganized with few resources and skills. They may be heavy consumers of alcohol, junk food, and lotteries. Televisions programs they might watch would include programs such as JeremyKyle. So, they may have relationship issues, and they might relate to this, and they might also read gossip magazines such as heat or reveal. And again the types of advert within these programs and magazines suit the audience they would be gambling or bingo, lottery, fast food, debt consolidation and things that offer instant solutions to their problems.

THE MAINSTREAMER

These would be domestic conformist, very conventional, sentimental, fairly passive and quite habitual. They like being part of the masses, and they're the biggest group that we see. The types of TV they would watch would be aimed at the mass audience, things like X-factor or Britain's Got Talent. Large brands would certainly advertise on these programs as they reach such a large audience. McDonald's or Coca-Cola, Nike and Adidas, those types of brands.

THE ASPIRER

These people are materialistic, acquisitive, so they're interested in acquiring stuff affiliative. So, they place importance on brands and identity, and they're oriented to intrinsic. So image, appearance, charisma, persona, and fashion. They feel the attractive packaging is more important than the quality of the contents. They might watch fashion programs, maybe the Brit Awards, Made in Chelsea or those type of programs but

HOW TO START A YOUTUBE CHANNEL FOR BEGINNERS. STANLEY P. CATHCART

mainly watch for the fashions and to compare themselves to the characters within the programs. And the types of adverts that we see within these programs are fashion items, beauty products, and anything related to the image.

THE SUCCEEDER.

They're very strong, goal orientated, confident, they've got a strong work ethic, they would support the status quo, and they like stability. They might like programs which confirm their position and status; one would be a wolf of Wall Street. But mainly programs where the main character will have flashy materialistic qualities. A good example would suit the series. And the adverts that we see within these programs are for luxury, prestigious and supposedly high-quality items.

THE EXPLORER

They are energetic, they have autonomy, and they go after an experience, challenge, and new frontiers. Their brand choices generally highlight different sensation, adventure, indulgence, and instant effect. They are supposedly the first to try new brands. These people are generally young, maybe students. They would probably appreciate programs about discovery or documentaries. They might like a program like Grand Designs.

HOW TO START A YOUTUBE CHANNEL FOR BEGINNERS. STANLEY P. CATHCART

The adverts you're likely to see in these sorts of programs are, adventure holidays, specific clothing brands and possibly Apple products suit these types of people.

THE REFORMER

These people have freedom from restriction, they value personal growth, social awareness, they put a value on time, they have very independent judgment, and they're anti-materialistic but intolerant of bad taste. They're curious and inquiring; they support the growth of new products and categories. They're mostly from a higher education background. They would probably watch programs that challenge them and build in some way, so documentaries, educational programs, political programs, and news. They're more likely to read a broadsheet newspaper because they're the reformer and anti-materialistic, you might find it hard to identify specific products that appear within the advert breaks. Items and products that have less emphasis on style and more emphasis on actual quality are likely candidates.

Some brands have these qualities, Volvo is a brand that places importance on building quality over an image, and there are other high-quality items. This combines with perhaps educational products. It can be seen from this that the four C's psychographic model can be an effective way of categorizing audiences.

It defines people through their personality and thinks about what might motivate them to watch or buy a media textile product. It's arguably a more useful method than the socio-economic groupings as it takes into account people's personality rather than just placing them into groups based on things like income and age, but you can probably see issues with this type of audience classification.

In this case, the terminology is quite derogatory and may be offensive, and it doesn't give the audience much credit. Looking at the list, you might feel that your personality does not fit into any of the categories. Therefore these groups defined here might have people missing, but this is an important aspect. Psychographics are changeable and adaptable, and these are simple groups defined by the young and rubican advertising agency.

There are other types designed by other people and groups. The U.S. vowels are a different psychographic model, still based on values, beliefs, opinions, and interests. But you can see from these groupings it has a little different approach with slightly different groupings.

Now we can apply psychographics to media texts without specifically thinking of advertising, so maybe thinking about the target audience of a film or a television program or a YouTube channel. So, let's look at romantic comedies or romance. Looking at the themes that we tend to see within this main genre characters often tend to be women struggling with love or looking for Mr. Right, and they go on a narrative of self-discovery and transformation. So this would possibly appeal to the struggler, and you can perhaps see films that relate to the other groups that we see in the list. Thus, the positives of psychographics is, it's possible to see how they're good at defining an aspect of the audience and it could be argued it's more precise than demographics at analyzing the behavior of viewers and consumers. The wrong point of psychographics is that it's based on qualitative data, so this cannot be quickly turned into charts or graphs.

HOW TO START A YOUTUBE CHANNEL FOR BEGINNERS. STANLEY P. CATHCART

CHAPTER FIVE

Getting familiar with your audience

How do you keep your current audience and subscribers engaged on YouTube? We've got five tips for you. It's challenging enough to build your subscriber base in the first place, but it's a whole different thing to keep them engaged. Just because someone subscribes originally to the video they might lose interest, they might get distracted. So, I wanted to share a few tips on why this is so important.

CONSISTENCY

It is so important to be consistently showing up in front of your subscribers not just on YouTube, on social media as well.

Especially in this busy world of social media and so many things come at people, you can get easily forgotten if you are not consistent. Along with consistency is conditioning. If people know you're showing up weekly, then they expect it, but if you miss a month, it's easy to be out of sight, out of mind. If you want to stay on top of the mind to keep your viewers engaged, stay consistent.

QUALITY IS BETTER THAN QUANTITY

Having said that about consistency, you want to have great content, you want to have content that people want to watch because this is a thing they love. If you've got a lot of uploads and people, don't want to watch it when it shows up in their subscription box they might not even click through. Have dope content that people want to watch. Your goal should be to create 'no missing' content now we get it. This is super hard, it's like the bar is always raising, and every single time you post a video you're really branding yourself, you're only as good as your last time at bat and if you put out a couple of videos that are really good for a while then your audience is like whoa they're dropping some really good videos. So, if you think about your best stuff on a scale from one to five, I like to say, never let your stuff drop below an four. If you can post videos two times a week and keep it at a four, maybe a three and half sometimes is cool. If you can go three times a week and do excellent work that is cool, but if you start posting too much and drops to a one or two ratings that speak to your audience and they can start disengaging.

ENGAGE

What we mean by this is to actually communicate with your audience, actually respond to comments. Go on social media and take the conversation to a deeper level that is what's going to keep people connected to your YouTube videos. Jump off the platform you might see someone in the comments on your YouTube channel, connect with them on Twitter. All of these touch points keep you again on top of mind and keep you engaged with your audience.

KEEP GROWING

It's a fact of life that some people lose interest, they're not going to YouTube anymore, and maybe their questions have been answered. So, it's significant always to find new subscribers that you can add value to. And if you go into your YouTube analytics every month, you'll notice that you gained some subscribers, but you also lost some. YouTube shut down a few accounts, they may be unsubscribed, and so you do need to be focusing on growth, progress, hustling grinding, because there's going to be attrition on every single YouTube channel.

FOCUSED CONTENT

What we're trying to say is don't get distracted. People subscribe for a specific reason, so like a Cooking Channel, they're subscribing for recipe videos. So, if out of nowhere you're doing like car reviews they're going to lose interest because the original reason why they subscribe is not being served. If you desire to keep your viewers engaged try to stay on brand. Keep leveling up, it doesn't mean you can't experiment but always consider that they showed up for one thing if you divert from that someone who subscribed might unsubscribe because your content is unfocused.

HOW TO START A YOUTUBE CHANNEL FOR BEGINNERS. STANLEY P. CATHCART

CHAPTER SIX

Producing high-quality videos. Value-based and content.

In this chapter, we're going to talk about the ingredients that make up a good video. So, these are specifically four tips that should help you know what should be the necessary things that you need to include in each of you YouTube videos to make sure that it's good and that it has an impact. And before we get into them, make sure you have a good foundation, a good start. Make sure you're talking about stuff that you're passionate about and that you know about because if you don't do those two things, then all these things don't matter. So, remember to do things you love when you're creating videos.

START OUT WITH A PURPOSE AND PLAN AHEAD OF TIME.

Preparation is key. So, some things that you can do when you're planning out a video is, ask questions from the audience and put some questions on social media to see what people are interested in. Research on Google if this is a topic that people even want to hear about. So, do Google keyword planner search, start typing search terms on YouTube to see if there's search around it. Is it something that people will like? So, you start off with planning and then having a purpose from the very beginning. You should be able to say what your video trying to achieve? Does it want to get views? Does it want to drive visitors to your website? If I have a business or a blog, does it want to promote a product, Get more subscribers?

What is the purpose of your video? Do you want to get a lot of comments, and likes and shares its entertainment and comedy? And are you trying to go viral with it? Start with a purpose in mind, and that helps you have a focus. So, a lot of content creators are more like a shotgun it spread wide as opposed to a laser just hitting one specific target, one video one focus, one purpose and it's more effective. And the second part is more on the technical side, to have Great video, great audio, and great lighting.

GREAT AUDIO.

One of the biggest things ever, actually probably more important than the video and what things look like, is having Good audio. If people can't hear it and they can't catch the nuances of the comedy or the detail of the person speaking, they will tolerate lower quality video but not necessarily audio, do what it takes to have good audio. And maybe like in some cases we recommended vlogging cameras. When it comes to audio, you might not be able to have an excellent microphone or something, but you can still shoot in a quiet place, in a non-echoed room, be close to your camera. Cars are a great place to shoot. So, think about the audio.

LIGHTING

Lighting may even be more important than the device you're shooting with because even with a phone camera you can get great video as long as your lights are pretty good. So, one thing that you need to do in the daily Vlogger is that you should make sure to shoot near windows; as much natural lighting as possible. It's incredible what kind of footage you can get outdoors when it's nice and sunny. And having all the lights on, let's say its night time there's no natural light, turn on all those lights no matter what device you're using. People are saying I want my Youtube videos to look better, what camera should I buy? And I would, almost nine times out of ten suggest that you invest in lighting and keep using the same camera even if it's just your smartphone. Good light will make it better. Actually, I will be talking about how to buy equipment for YouTube videos for less than $90 in the next chapter. So, now your video has a purpose, it has a focus, you've got good audio, you've got good video, here's the most important thing.

HOW TO START A YOUTUBE CHANNEL FOR BEGINNERS. STANLEY P. CATHCART

ADDING VALUE

This may come in different forms. If you are an informative channel, giving good information, educating your viewers. Say you're an entertainment channel, whether it's comedy, whether you're a vlogger, whether you're a travel person, like giving great entertainment and giving value so that those people are being entertained at the moment from your videos. And another way is connecting. A lot of people want to connect with you as a person. And so let me just run these down off of a list and connect these all the way back to the purpose of your video. You should say from the beginning that your video is trying to do one of these things.

1. Connection, building a community. Maybe you're doing something collaborative, and you're focused on specifically building a community. That's what YouTube is all about, is a community. So, that becomes the purpose of your video.

HOW TO START A YOUTUBE CHANNEL FOR BEGINNERS. STANLEY P. CATHCART

2. Entertainment, like comedy. You should have decided if your channel is going to be entertaining or it's going to be hilarious.

3. Inspiration. You could say I'm setting up this video to inspire people in an area, to spark motivation, to spark, to inspire.

4. Motivation: Maybe you're trying to motivate people. And so, you have a fitness channel, and you're motivating people to weight loss, or you're trying to encourage people that don't think that they could be good at editing videos or creating videos to go out and crush it with creating videos.

5. Information: News - It could just be news. Here's the latest, here's some info, the purpose of this video is to share some information.

6. To solve a problem: You create a video that solves people's problems. This is happening all the time. Solve a problem, share your answers to a problem. So at purpose stage, you're like this video is going to solve this problem for people.

7. It's going to educate people. And if you're going to educate, you need to make sure you know your stuff. Yes, you have to be experienced on what you're talking about. If you set out to educate and you're not teaching well, and you haven't developed expertise, maybe you shouldn't be creating videos like that yet.

And the reason is delivering value, whatever that value is, is so important and probably supersedes the other two points whether it's the technical side of it or the preparation or the other things that make a good video, is because especially with devices they're getting so simple when I say devices with apps and platforms like Snapchat, Twitter, and Facebook video.

You don't need a lot of stuff, and you don't need to prepare to deliver Value, and that's why I think it's more important now more than ever to make sure that's what you're doing and to focus on that which brings you again full circle to what you're passionate about and what you know the best.

HOW TO START A YOUTUBE CHANNEL FOR BEGINNERS. STANLEY P. CATHCART

Lastly, you learn by doing. So, you should continuously work on making your videos better. In conclusion, get started and learn as you go. Always seek to level your videos up, try to make it look better, try to make it sound better, try to make the content better, to teach better. If you're always growing, then your audience is going to grow with you, and you're going to have an enormous impact and build your influence with video.

CHAPTER SEVEN

Getting your video equipment for less than $90

People always ask me what equipment I use or what camera they should get to start a YouTube channel. This chapter will show you how to make a YouTube video with a budget of only $95. I will be showing you some equipment you can get on Amazon for less than $95 for your videos, and you will get quality videos. The content of a video is always more important than video quality as I have already said in the previous chapter. You could have the best video quality in the world, but it wouldn't mean anything if you didn't have good content behind it. But at the same time, a lot of good content can be ruined by blurry video, bad audio or bad lighting.

This chapter will hopefully show you how to make your videos to your fullest potential.

Let's start with the camera, what people always ask for the most. I've said this before, but I think that audio quality and lighting are more important than a super high-resolution 4k camera with tons of features. So, I haven't put any of the $95 budget towards the camera. Most people don't know that the video quality from recent smartphones is often as good as or even better than some $200 cameras. You can record with your iPhone 7, but any smartphone that can film in 1080p should do the trick. For example, you can start your channel with Galaxy s4 smartphone that filmed in 1080p, and nobody will ever complain about the video quality. You can add color correction to the video. You can head to YouTube to learn how to color correct a video that will not be covered in this book.

MINI PHONE TRIPOD

You'll need something to set your phone on to film yourself and can use a makeshift stand maybe lean it up against the shoe or something. But for only $5 you can get this mini phone tripod that is shown below, and it makes things a lot easier.

TONOR Professional Studio Condenser Microphone Computer PC Microphone Kit

Let's move on to audio. The audio setup I'm using right here is from a company called toner. Now they have a killer value for a complete setup that comes with the microphone itself, a suspension boom arm, a shock mount, a windscreen and a pop filter all for just $25. The mic, the boom arm, and shock mount are all built with metal and feel premium and durable. So, this is an XLR mic but it comes with an XLR to 3.5-millimeter jack and a USB plugin so you can use it directly to a computer, or you could plug it into a portable recorder like the team dr-40. Like I said the audio quality is fascinating for the price. $25 for this whole setup is a great deal.

TESCAM DR-40

FOUR SOCKET SOFTBOX

Moving on to lighting, I've got a pretty simple setup going on right here. So, for $35 you can get a four-socket softbox that comes with the reflector and the four-socket adapter, and you can put all that on a cheap light stand adjustable tripod from Bay that cost only about $10.

four socket softbox

Light stand Adjustable Tripod for Softboox Flashing Lighting Kit

You're also going to need some nice bright light bulbs to go with that setup, and you can get a 2-pack of 85watt daylight fluorescent light bulbs for only $17. You can get four of these bulbs obviously because there are four sockets on the softbox which would be ideal but that would push us over the budget, so for now, we're only using two.

2 x 85W
Energy Saving Bulb

Hopefully, this chapter has taught you that you don't need a huge budget to make high-quality videos. As long as you've got the three basics of audio quality, lighting, and video quality, you should be good to go.

CHAPTER EIGHT

Editing your videos with Shortcut free software.

I know that a lot a people that start a YouTube channel begins with a low budget. Because of this, I have looked for software that will help you edit your video without paying through your nose and the software is called Shortcut.

How can I edit this one-minute clip, I forgot to turn off my camera and was picking my nose the entire time. Shortcut: the easiest video editing software you'll ever use I promise. Let's do it. I want to show you the program that I use to edit my video, and mix videos with my audio and intro and everything it is completely free, 100% free. It's an open source

74

program called shortcut some of you may have heard of it. It is the easiest program I have ever used. So, first of all, you're going to go to Google the website is www.shotcutapp.com.   Once you get to the page you're going to click and download it, and then get it installed. Once you got it installed, open it up.

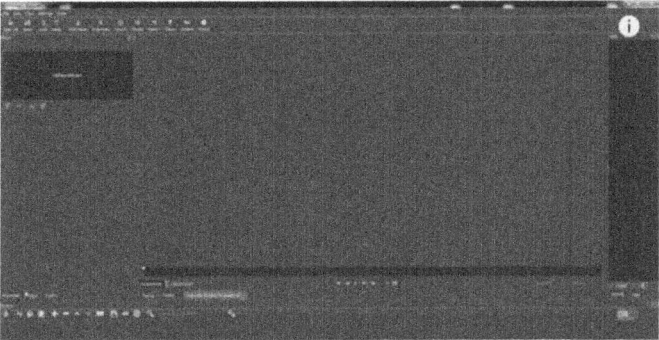

Once you get it opened up, the first thing you want to do is you want to add your timeline which is going to be your audio, video.

Creating your timeline

The first thing you have to do is to set up your timeline. If you open the shortcut app and you can't see the timeline, this is what to do. Click on "**view**", from the drop-down menu click on "**timeline**". So, what you have to do is to first click on where the arrow is pointing at in the image below and select "**Add audio track**."

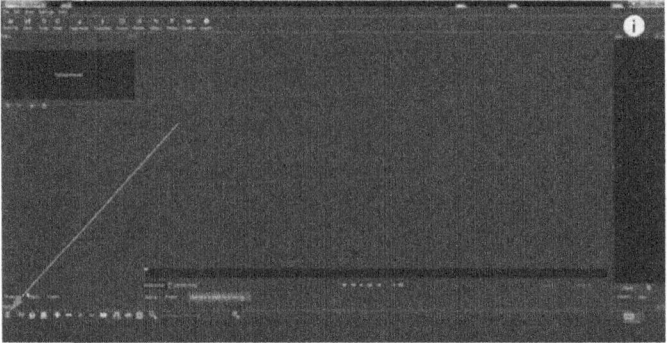

Still, click where the arrow is pointing and select "**Add video track**" to add your video track to the timeline. If you have intro recorded separately, you will need to add it up too. Once you are done creating your timeline, click on "**Open file**" to import your files. Look at the image below.

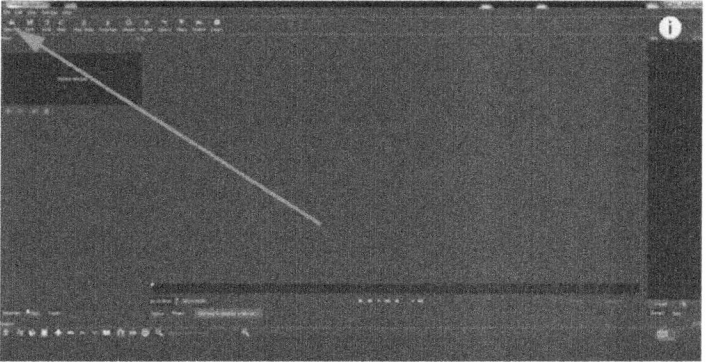

Open up the video you want to edit, then click on the video and drag it to the timeline. Repeat the same thing for all the files you will like to edit. Now you have to arrange the files the way you want them to play. Simply click and drag the video or audio to the position you want them to be. The one placed first will play first followed by the one place second and so on. You have to know that if you allow your entire file lined up vertically in a straight line, it's not going to be great, all of them will pay at the same time, and that is not what you want. After assembling your video on your timeline, play your video to see how it will play out.

Next thing you're probably wondering is, what if I got a section of the video that I don't want in there because I wasted time where I was transitioning between my camera and something else and I need to cut out that part of my video.

It is as simple as this, all you're going to do is you're going to get to that point where you want to cut out of your video. Be sure to select the video you want to cut some part out before doing this. Once you are in the area you want to cut out, click on the icon the arrow below is pointing at.

Cutting out the edge of the videos.

If your video did not start well or end well and you will like to cut section of your video before you begin editing, this is what you need to do. Immediately after you open the file, you will see that end where the blue arrows are pointing at in the picture below.

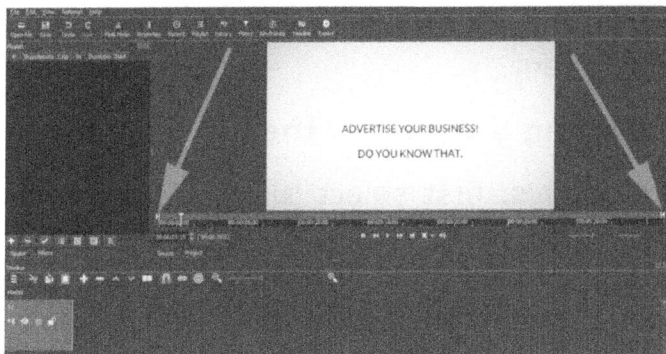

Click on that arrow with a straight line attached to it and drag to where you want to cut out of your video. You can do this for both sides of the video. Like it is shown in the image below.

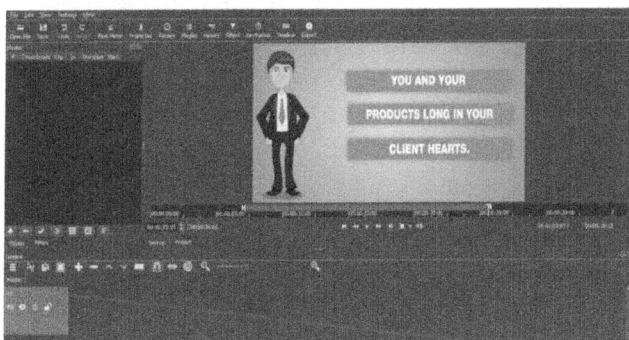

Then click on the video hold down and drag to your timeline. Once you have done this, you can go to cut out part of the video that is inside your video that you don't want.

Cutting out part of the inside video.

To do this, first select the audio or video you want to cut out part it. In this case, we have only one video, so select the video then look for the part you want to cut out by bringing the play line to the spot. Look at the picture below for better understanding.

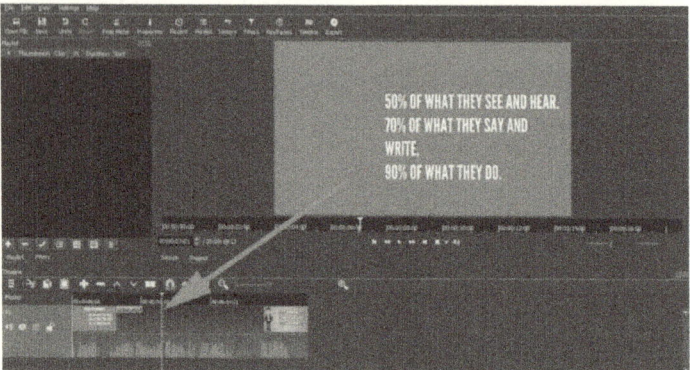

Drag that play line to the point in the video you want to cut out. Then click on that icon that the arrow is pointing at in the image below to spit it up.

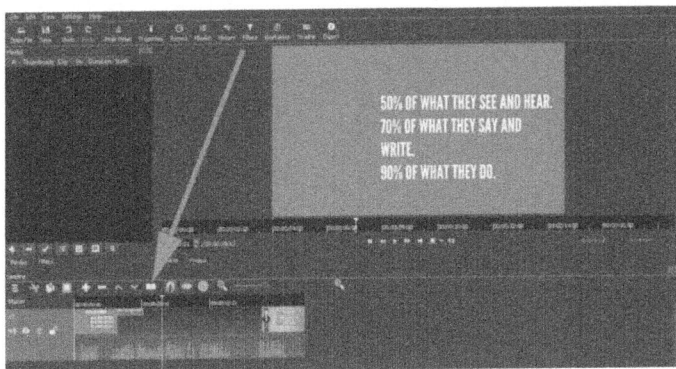

When you click on that icon, it splits up into two. Repeat the same thing with your audio files to match up your content. Click the play line again, hold down and drag to the area you want to cut. Click on that icon where the arrow is pointing on the image above again or use the shortcut S. Click inside the area you have selected to cut, then click on the letter X which will delete the section of the video you don't want.

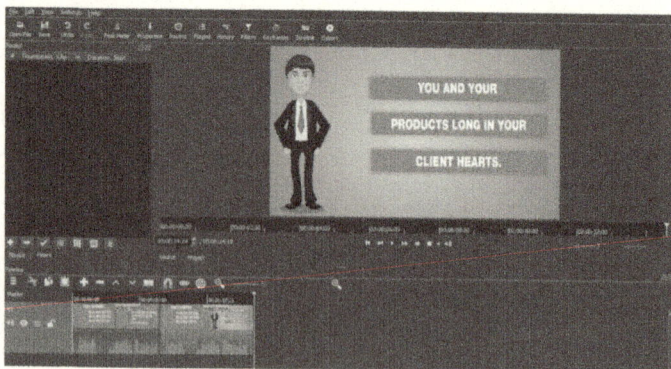

As you can see from the picture above, the section of the video we don't want has been removed.

Note: If you are working on a video and you make an error or did what you don't like, click on CTRL+Z to return you to where you were before the mistake.

Adding text to your video.

Select the part of the video you want to write on by dragging the play line to the place you want the word to start from. Slit the pay head again by pressing the letter S, then drag your play line to where you want your text to stop and split the play head again. Then select the portion of the video you want the text to show up, then

HOW TO START A YOUTUBE CHANNEL FOR BEGINNERS. STANLEY P.
CATHCART

make sure filter is selected. You can do
this by clicking in any of the places the
two arrows in the image below is pointing
at.

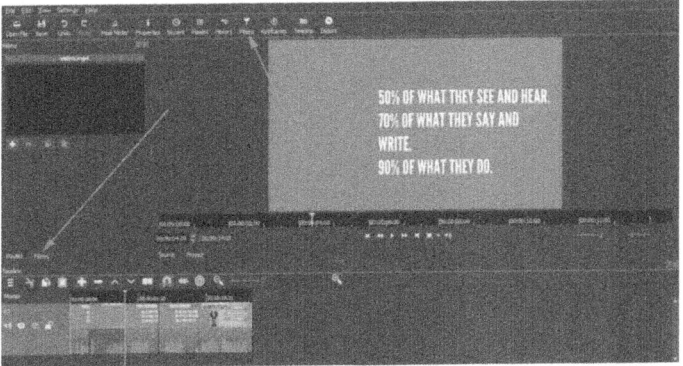

Then go ahead and click on the plus
button which is the add button. When you
click on that button this is what you see:

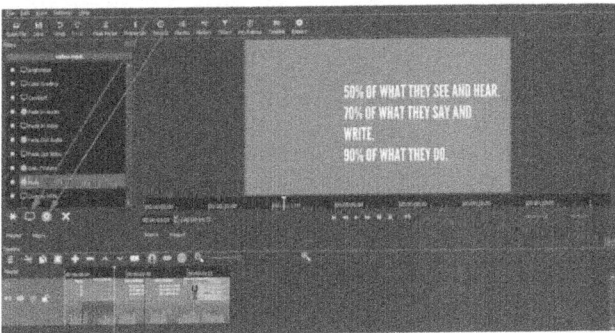

The red arrow is pointing at the video filter while the blue arrow is pointing at the audio filter. Since we are working with video and we want to write on our video, click on the video filter. You can either choose the 3d text, or you scroll down to select the normal text.

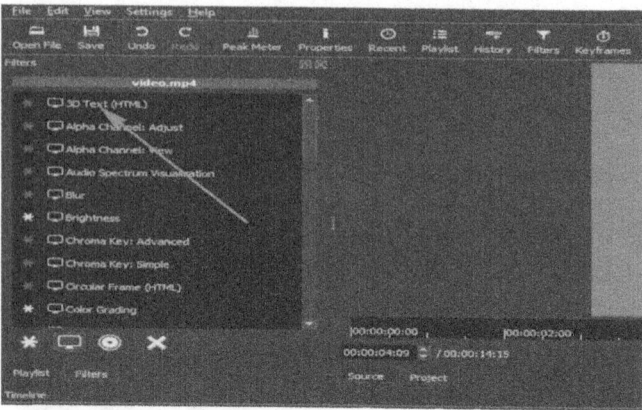

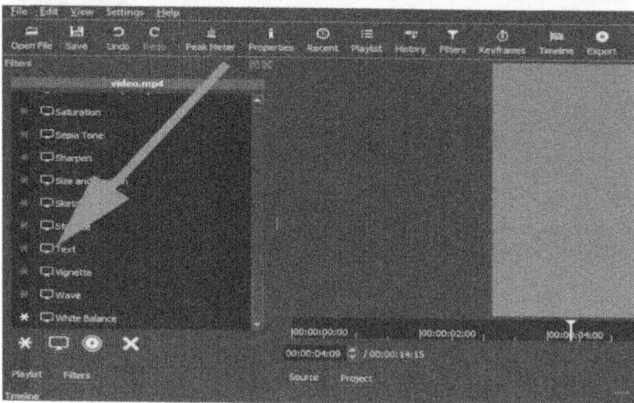

HOW TO START A YOUTUBE CHANNEL FOR BEGINNERS. STANLEY P. CATHCART

You can see that the text box has taken the entire screen.

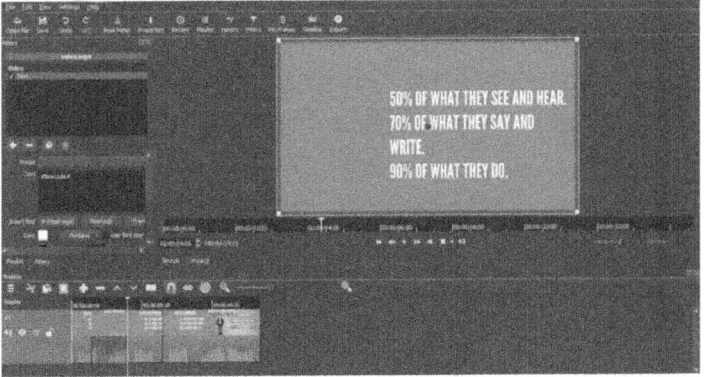

Click and drag the small white rectangular box by the edge of the large rectangular text box and drag to reposition to where you want your text to be.

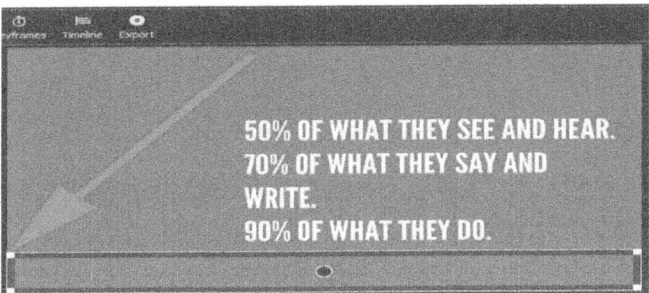

Click on that small rectangular box the arrow is pointing at, hold down and drag to reposition your text box to where you want the text to be. To move the text box around the screen, you will need to click on the small circle at the middle of the text box, hold down and drag to wherever you want it to be. Then go to the text box, high light and delete whatever is there and type what you want. When you do that you will discover that the text appears in the box as you type. When you scroll down, you will see all the properties you need to change the color of your text and format your text as you want.

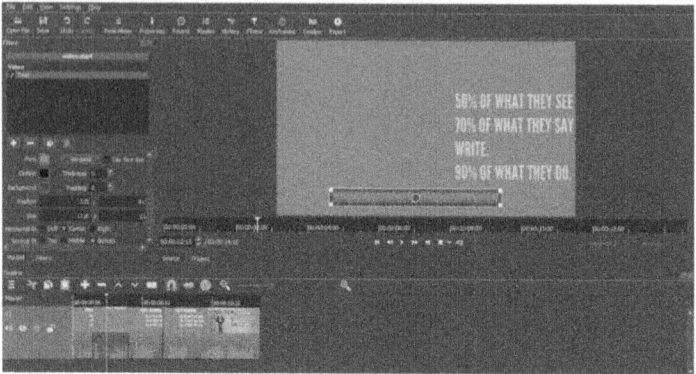

As you can see, I have clicked on the font and change the color of my text to Red. This is like that. Go back to your video now and play it and see how it plays out.

Adding filters to your video

Assuming you want to fade in your video, this is what you need to do, select the part of the video you want to fade in and click on the plus button on the filter again and select fade in.

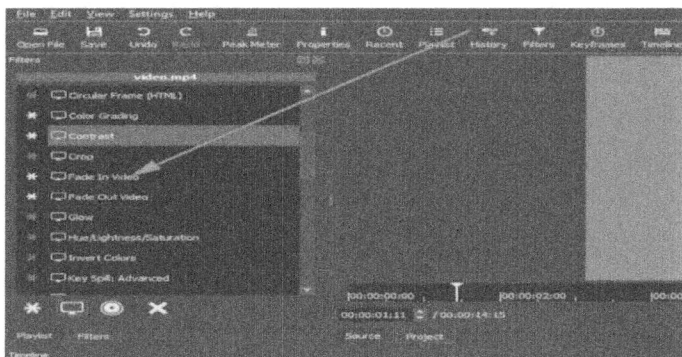

You can repeat the same for the part of any video you want to fade out.

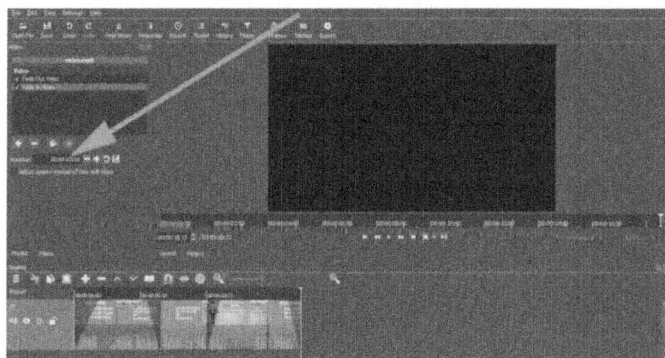

Click on where the arrow is pointing to set the time for the fade in and fade out.

Before you set the duration for the fade in and fade out you must first click on the one you want to set the duration in the text box, or you set the duration immediately you add the fade in or fade out.

You can see that this is very simple to use. As you use this software consistently, you will get to know it better and will find out many features in the application that we have not touched.

Exporting your video for use.

Once you are satisfied with your video, you can export it for use. What you have to do is go to file menu, click on "**Export video**." The settings that I recommend is to go the where you see the arrow on the image below.

That is the setting for the video that I
recommend for you. You can leave the
settings to the right-hand side the way
there are. Click on the file format and
select whichever format you want, but the
mp4 format works well, so I recommend it
to you.

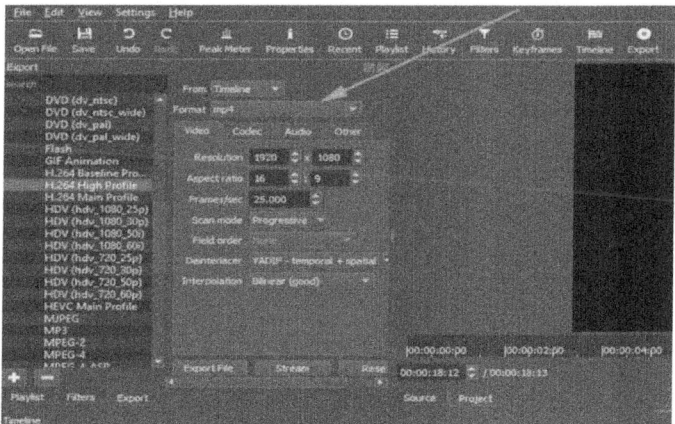

HOW TO START A YOUTUBE CHANNEL FOR BEGINNERS. STANLEY P.
CATHCART

Click on codec and make sure that the '**libx264**' is selected. You can also increase the quality to 70% or more. Once you are done with your entire selection click on the "**Export file**", name your file and click "**save**".

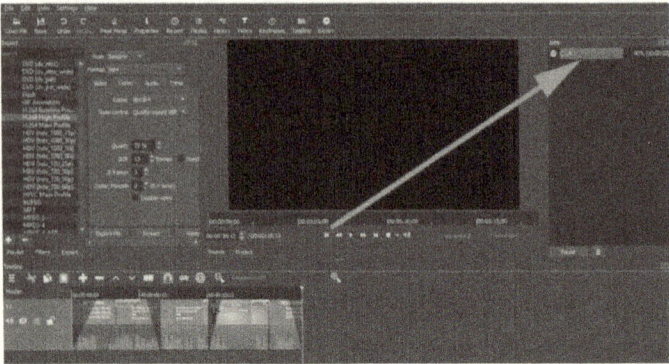

You can see from the top right of that image that it is being exported and it's already at 90%. Once it is done, you can go to where the file is saved and play it and see what you have done.

Congratulations, you have just learned how to use shortcut free software to edit your video professionally. You can do whatever you want to do with this application as you get used to it. If you want to learn more about this application or there are something's that you need more clarification on, head over to YouTube and learn more.

CHAPTER NINE

How to upload your video

Many don't know the right way of uploading a video to a YouTube channel for it to be found by the public. Many that know does it the wrong way, and this chapter and the next will show you exactly what to do to get it right. So, my question to you is, are you doing it right? Are your videos being found and watched? If not, this chapter and next is for you. I will show you how to upload a video to YouTube plus I will show you what YouTube deems as necessary. Let's take a look.

To upload that video the first thing that you need to do is to sign in to YouTube.

HOW TO START A YOUTUBE CHANNEL FOR BEGINNERS. STANLEY P. CATHCART

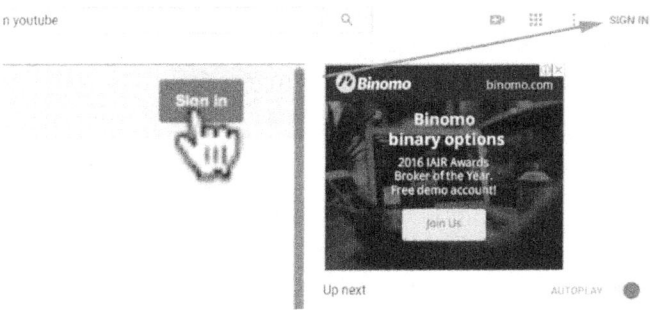

So go up here and click on "**SIGN IN**" and log in. Now that we're logged in, right at the top, you're going to see an icon and all you need to do is click on it and then click on Upload. See the images below.

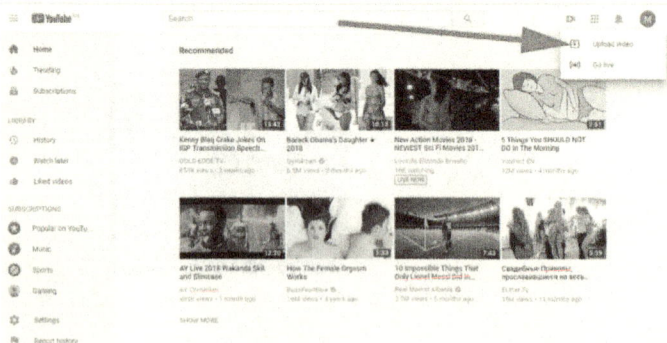

It's going to bring you up to this page right below, and you can either drag and drop your files here, and it will start to upload, or you can click on it.

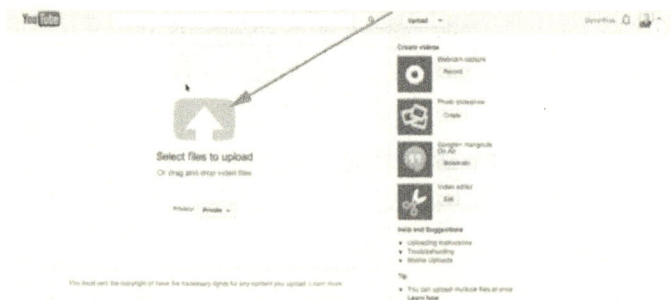

Go ahead and click on "select files to upload". This will take to where you can upload your file from your desktop or wherever you have it located. It is going to bring you to this page while it's uploading.

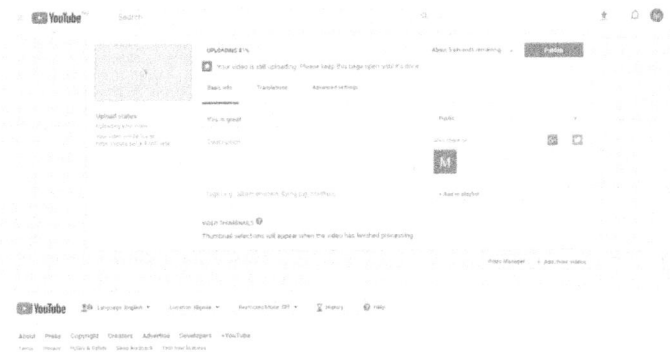

This is where you need to put in all your information of how people are going to find you.

The next chapter, which is chapter ten, covers effectively how to fill in the data in the tag and description for proper optimization.

While you are still working on your file, you can decide to keep it in the privacy settings as shown below.

New Hummingbird Search

Uploading your video, 2 minutes remaining. Your video will be live at http://youtu.be/4t6117kuC2g

                                                          + Add to ▾   ✕ Cancel

Basic info   Monetization   Advanced settings

Title

New Hummingbird Search Algorithm Changes

Description

SCHEDULE

Mondays
Facebook Training
http://www.youtube.com/playlist?list=PLVODYj2uxE8fikXAde8hQuKhz33Dz8b3zP
Google+ Training
http://www.youtube.com/playlist?list=PLVODYi2uxE8fivnUkoJAOk9OG7K-KusTx6

Public
Unlisted
Private
Scheduled

Category

Howto & Style

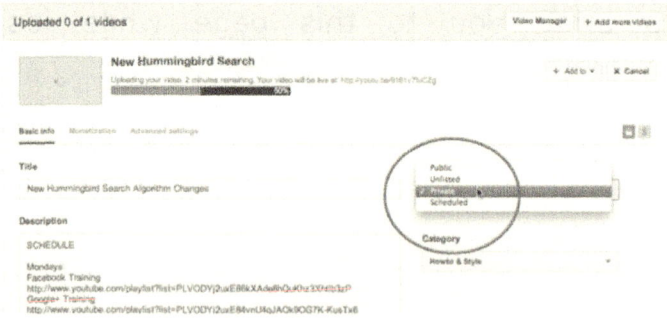

There are four options inside the circle that you can work with. Let's explain what these options will do one after the other.

1. Public: You can decide to set your YouTube upload directly to the public. What this means is that your content will be published to the public immediately you hit the publish button.

2. Unlisted: I like this feature so much, with this feature you can save all your video on YouTube and give access to only the people you want to watch the video. Only people who know the link to the video or people you decide to send the link to can view it. They could be your friends, family, or well-wishers. An unlisted video will not appear in any of YouTube's public spaces.

3. Private: This helps you to keep your videos private. You may not want the public to see your video while you are still working on it, and then use this option. You might even decide to keep it completely private. This is entirely up to you.

4. Schedule: This is an essential option which can help you to work ahead of time. You might decide to schedule many videos you want to publish to a future date. This option is excellent because it allows you to take a break and your videos will still be posted as of when due because you have scheduled the video to display at a specific date.

Add to Playlist

You will see add to playlist inside the circle in the image shown below. If you are starting your channel newly, you may not have any add to playlist.

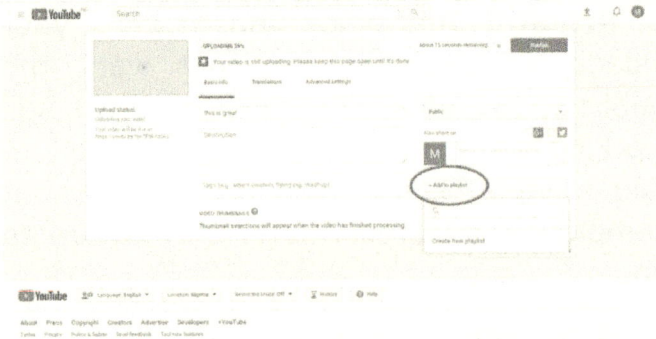

There are two ways of creating this.

1.   You can click on the plus sign beside the "**ADD TO PLAYLIST**" and create your playlist. Give it whatever name you want it to have and save it

2.   Secondly, YouTube can generate the playlist for you based on the YouTube you have watched and liked over the years.

Last step, all you need to do is double check your work and change your privacy setting from private to public and hit Publish.

Once you hit the publish button your video will be released to the public. Be sure to follow all the optimization process you will see in chapter ten for your videos to be found. It's of no good publishing a video that nobody will watch unless if you want it private.

Congratulation! You now know how to upload a video to YouTube. Let's move on to how you can optimize your YouTube video for many people to see it without necessarily spending money in advertising your videos.

CHAPTER TEN

Optimizing your YouTube channels.

If you want your video to be seen easily, you need to understand what SEO or YouTube SEO is. If you don't understand this and don't play the game according to the set rules, you will have videos that nobody will watch because it cannot be found. Producing video without people watching it is not good for any YouTube channel at all.

In this chapter, I'm going to show you how you can rank your video on the first page of YouTube and start getting the views and subscribers that your channel deserves. But before I begin, I want to go into what is YouTube SEO and how can you take advantage of YouTube SEO. SEO stands for search engine optimization so

100

basically what you're going to be doing is you're going to be optimizing your YouTube video to show on the first page of YouTube in Google. Now when you do this, two things are going to happen,

1. People are going to be able to find your video

2. You're going to get an influx of subscribers because more people are going to be checking out your videos.

In this chapter, I'm going to give you five practical tips on how to do this, and I'm going to walk you through exactly how to do it, so you don't get lost in the system.

KEYWORD RESEARCH.

What is your video about? What are you trying to do? Who are you trying to target and what keyword are you going for. Because a lot of times people will make a YouTube video name it a random keyword as if it's the case with ash tag and all of a sudden your video is not ranking. What's vital for you to do is, if you have a smaller channel make sure that you are doing keyword research. I'm going to show you how to do that right now.

We will be looking for long tail keywords. And what I mean by a long tail keyword is a keyword that's more than three keywords. Long tail keywords would be anything that's a little longer than normal. I'm going to give you an example. This is a short tail keyword "YouTube SEO" right. So, this is a little keyword not big it's two characters long. And here's something that would be a long tail "YouTube SEO 2018" this would be a long tail keyword. So this means that it's less competitive there are fewer people going for this type of keyword, this is the keyword that you want to go ahead and optimize for. What you don't want to do is, you don't want to optimize your YouTube video for this keyword because this is a very big keyword with a lot of searches per month, but you may want to search for something like "how to do SEO for tiny website" that is a good long tail keyword you can probably rank for that. This little section of this book is going to teach you exactly how to do some long tail keyword research. I like to use https://ubersuggests.io. The reason why I like this tool is that it uses the Google Suggest as you can see from the image below.

The Google suggest keyword are those dropdown sentences you see when you type in your keyword as shown above.

The reason why I like this is that user suggest is pulling the data right from there. Let's say we were trying to rank this YouTube SEO video and I wanted to find keyword.

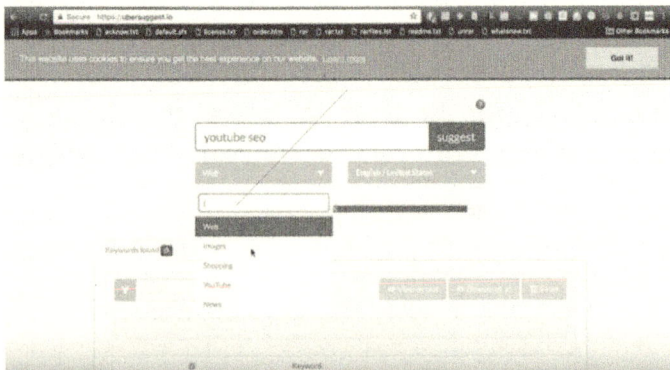

Type in "YouTube SEO" as shown in the picture above and then click where the arrow is pointing at, you will see the down suggestions, click on the YouTube. Then go ahead and click on the word "**suggestion**" to the right of the YouTube SEO you typed.

What this tool is going to do is, it's going to recommend a bunch of different keywords for us and give us some keyword ideas. So, that's going to make it a lot easier for us to rank in the search engines.

Keyword	Monthly Volume	CPC	Competition			
▼ youtube seo	12,100	$2.22	0.16	12,100	$2.22	0.16
▼ youtube seo tips	720	$1.42	0.06	720	$1.42	0.06
▼ youtube seo hindi	0	$0.00	0	0	$0.00	0
▼ youtube seo bangla	0	$0.00	0	0	$0.00	0
▼ youtube seo telugu	0	$0.00	0	0	$0.00	0
▼ youtube seo software	260	$3.47	0.3	260	$3.47	0.3
▼ youtube seo tricks	30	$0.27	0.02	30	$0.27	0.02
▼ youtube seo tool	1,000	$3.48	0.25	1,000	$3.48	0.25
▼ youtube seo store	20	$0.00	0.2	20	$0.00	0.2
▼ youtube seo tags	0	$0.00	0	0	$0.00	0

We've gotten the results. We have YouTube SEO, YouTube SEO tips, and it also gives you the monthly volume.

Keyword	Monthly Volume	CPC	Competition			
▼ youtube seo course	40	$1.04	0.28	40	$1.04	0.28
a						
▼ youtube seo algorithm	10	$0.00	0.02	10	$0.00	0.02
▼ youtube seo apk	0	$0.00	0	0	$0.00	0
▼ youtube seo automation	0	$0.00	0	0	$0.00	0
▼ youtube seo and best tag description	0	$0.00	0	0	$0.00	0
▼ youtube video seo and how to rank higher in youtube	0	$0.00	0	0	$0.00	0
▼ youtube seo tips and tricks	0	$0.00	0	0	$0.00	0
▼ youtube video seo optimized and marketing	0	$0.00	0	0	$0.00	0
▼ youtube seo ayanfe	0	$0.00	0	0	$0.00	0
▼ youtube seo arias	0	$0.00	0	0	$0.00	0

Let go ahead choose the long tail keyword that the cursor is pointing at- "YouTube video SEO and how to rank higher in YouTube" So, go ahead and copy this keyword and make sure that this keyword is going to work with your video. Make this keyword the title of your video.

You can go in and start looking at these keywords and pick the one that you want to optimize your video for. I highly recommend you stay away from anything that is above 300 search volume because there's a likely high change that you're not going to rank for something like that. But you also want to pick a keyword that has a lot of titles in it, or a lot of descriptions in it, especially if you're a smaller channel because it's way more likely that you're going to rank for that. So we're going to take this keyword, and we're going to go on to the next steps.

FILE OPTIMIZATION

So, once we found the keyword that we want to rank for, the next thing we're going in to look- is file optimization, which basically means when we upload videos onto YouTube, we got to make sure that YouTube knows what the video is about and the best way to do that is actually by starting with your file.

I'm going to show you how you're going to optimize this file for the keyword we just chose. Because we want to choose a long tail keyword, remember we're not a big YouTube channel, we don't have a lot of subscribers yet, and we also want to name the file that long tail keyword. So, let me show you how to do that right now.

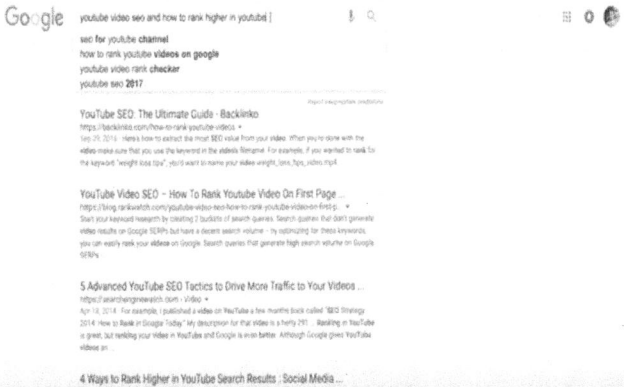

We're back. If you just read my explanation of the file and how to name your file before you go ahead and upload the YouTube, remember that this is our money keyword. So, copy this keyword and before we even upload to YouTube follow this simply steps.

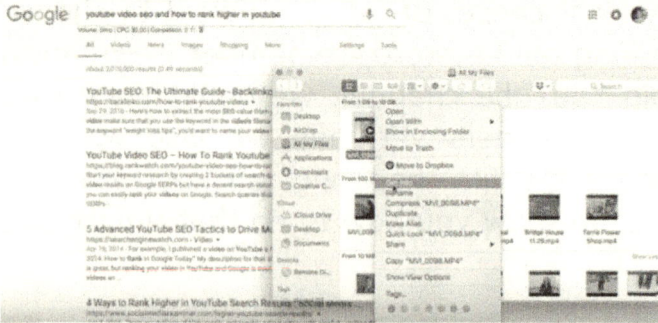

Take a video file, right-click if you're on Windows, and double click here on Mac, go on to "**get info**" and make sure that that keyword is in your tag, paste the keyword you have copied there.

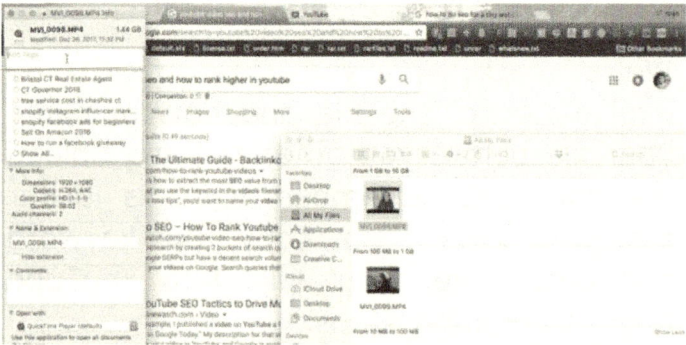

Make sure it's in your comment section too. A lot of people overlook this part. And then also make sure it's the title of your video. So, by doing this, it's going to give YouTube a signal that your video is about what it's about. And this is one of the signals that we're going to send to YouTube, and we're also going to send a lot more, but this is how you optimize your file. You want to name it in there, and it'll start ranking on the first page. So guys make sure you go ahead and click on the get info on Mac or Windows and then name your keyword what you're going for before you do the upload. When you go ahead and do the upload, you'll notice that the file you want to upload is named the title of the keyword. So, go ahead and upload it.

LONG VIDEOS DO BETTER.

Now that we've got our keyword, we know what we're going to be talking about; we've already made the video. What I want to make sure that you understand is that long-form videos tend to do better. If you've ever searched for anything on YouTube, you'll notice that the best-viewed videos are the ones that are 10 minutes or more. The reason why is because YouTube is confident that your video is going to get more watched time if it's longer because there's more content built into it. So I would recommend that you make a longer video. Now you've made your video hopefully its long form. Hopefully, it's 10 minutes long, or 3 minutes long, whatever you want to make it. If it's an instructional video make sure it's 10 minutes.

TITLE AND TAG OPTIMIZATION

Now, what we're going to look into, are your title and your tag optimization? We have the long tail keyword. We've already picked a long tail keyword. Now we've already optimized the file, we've made the video, and it's nice and long. The next thing we're going to do is we're going to upload it onto YouTube. We're going to change the title to maximize your keyword. I'm going to show you how to fluff in the tags in there, so you start ranking for not only one keyword but more a lot more keywords, like a couple of videos of mine, are ranking for 20 keywords. So, that's what you want with every single video, and I promise you-

you're going to see substantial growth in your YouTube channel. I'm going to show you exactly how I do this, and some examples that I've seen in the past that have helped me grow. So let's take a look into it.

Once you've gotten the long-form video, you are about to upload it you will see this page.

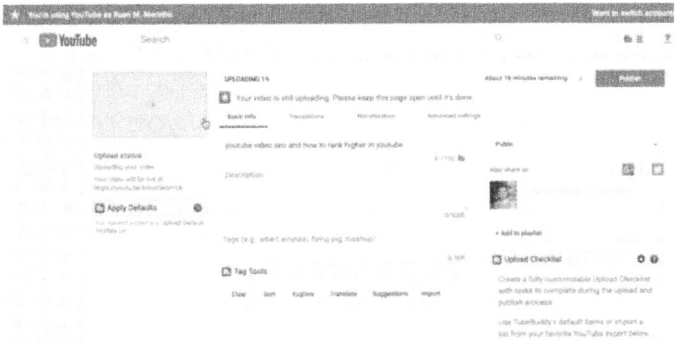

Now I'm going to show you how to rank number one for this keyword. So, what you're going to do is you're immediately going to copy the long tail keyword and put it as a first tag as shown below. See the blue arrow.

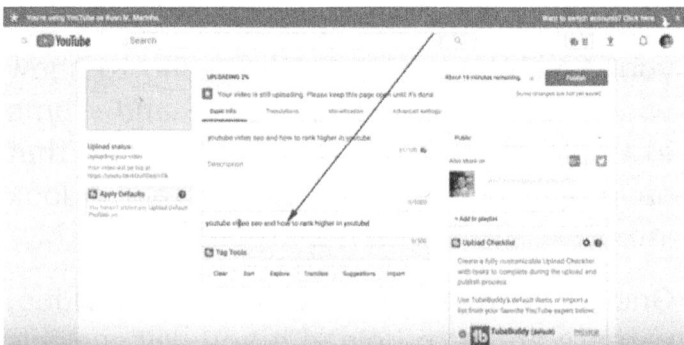

The reason is that YouTube now knows the title of your video, they also want to know that it's your tag, and you're also going to want to put it first in your description where the blue arrow is pointing.

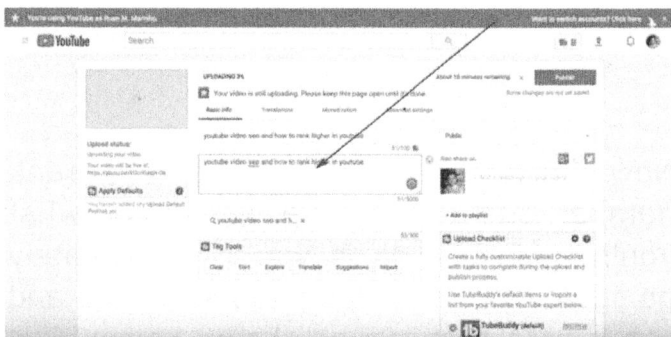

Put in the little dash and then start typing your description. What's essential about the description is used at least 500

characters in your description. Don't just do the keyword and then leave it. YouTube's looking at this long-form stuff, and they're making sure that you are keeping on top of this. This is important as well as the translations and the transcribing of your video. I'm going to show you how to optimize your tags to rank for multiple keywords.

Every tag you should make should have a keyword that is in your title. What do I mean by that? You want to create variations of this stuff because it's going to help you rank for more keywords. Look at the image below.

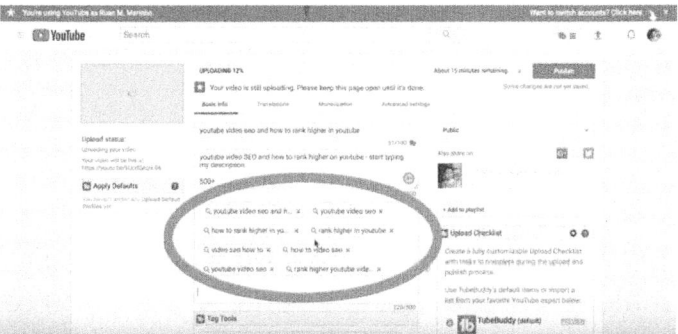

The more you do this, the more keywords you're going to rank for.

Now the other thing that you need to do which is important is, take these keywords and sprinkled them into your description. Try as much as you can to get these keywords in your description. It might be difficult because, it won't look natural. But I think you guys get the gist here. It's straightforward to do this, and as long as you keep on doing this with consistency on your YouTube videos, you'll see a large amount of growth. I want to make this very clear that you make sure you sprinkle in your title in different variations of the keyword in your tags and you will see some tremendous results. That is it. That's how you do the titles, the tags, everything's good to go, so you want to make sure you upload it.

ENGAGEMENT

I want you to also think about when you're making these videos and when you're uploading them about engagement. How can you get people to engage with you? I'm going to show you a few different examples of people who do an excellent job in engagement, and maybe you can take those and implement them in your channel. If you don't have a lot of money, don't worry about this yet because it does cost money to get this type of engagement. But if you are starting, you might want to ask provoking questions throughout your content to get people to respond down below.

Let me show you a few different examples of how people are getting some engagement, and you can tailor that to your strategy and go from there. We are now talking about how some of these bigger YouTubers get engagement on their videos. And we're going to start naturally right now which is enforcing engagement because I could see YouTuber in the future saying, hey you can't force engagement by running contests, let's look at Neil Patel. Neil Patel is one of the most successful search engine optimizations. I would say he is a guru out there, an entrepreneur. He owned several software companies, and I want you to look at his style here.

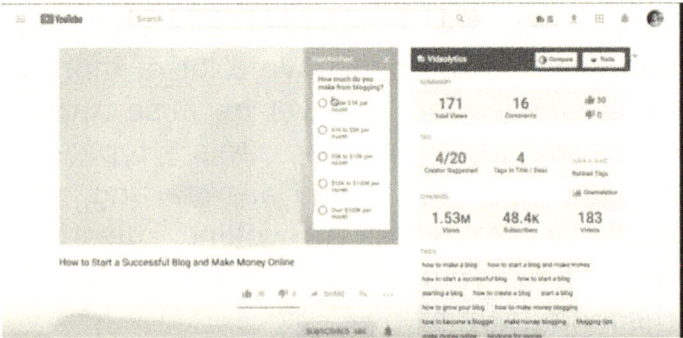

He puts out great content, and then he asks questions in this little side tab. And you can click where the red arrow is pointing and as you can see it gets engagement.

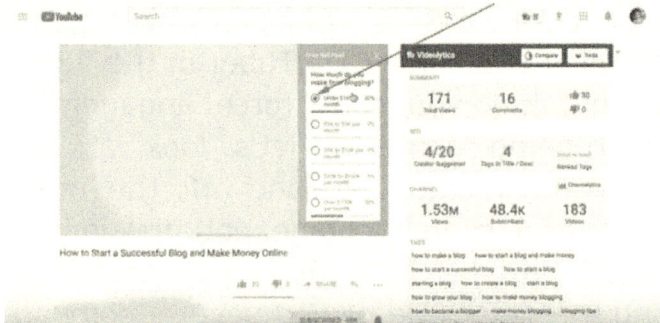

But it also sparks conversation in the comment section. As you can see below.

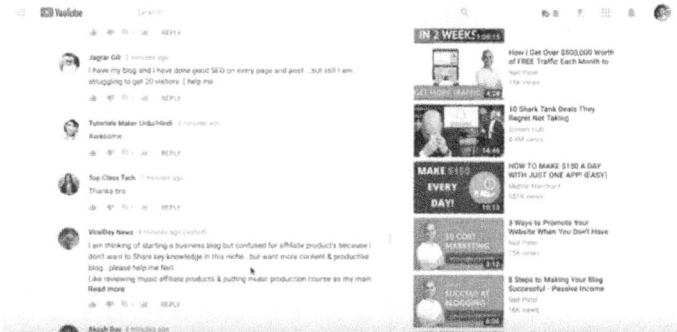

The other thing Neil does well is to make sure that he comments back to almost every person who comments. What this does is, it gets people to go ahead and comment on your newer videos driving more engagement. If people responded in the past and you answered a very tough question for them, they're going to be more open to comment on your videos in the future. Neil is excellent about this. I do not know if he's responding or his team's responding, I don't know, I do know that Neal is excellent about this kind of stuff.

I hope this example has shown you practically how to engage with your viewers.

CONCLUSION

Congratulations! You have prepared the groundwork for making money with YouTube by putting to practice what you read in this book from beginning to end. The world will never reward you for what you know but for what you have done. So, start putting this into practice now if you have not started and be very diligent about it.

The part two and three of this book will show you precisely how to monetize your YouTube channel for greater profit. You can go ahead and get the part two and three of this book. It was written in a simple language and easy to understand steps which can help you make money from YouTube. Due to the many things you need to learn about YouTube, I have taken it upon myself to give you a very balanced knowledge. So, learn practice until it becomes easy for you to produce a professional video within a very short period of time.